# INVESTMENT FOR BEGINNERS

A practical beginner's guide to the main investments available and how
to start your path to a better financial future

Marcella Sersante

# Disclaimer:

The contents in this book are for information purposes only. Always do your own diligence first before investing to ensure you understand the risks.

# Copyright:

# Table of Contents

# INTRODUCTION

You work hard for your money. Now it is time to make your money work hard for you!

Leaving your money dormant in some savings account is not the only option out there, and you must know that.

You should know what investment opportunities are available to you and what each of them entails.

As a non-financial person, it can be tough to understand financial terms and how you can apply them. It can be scary enough to put some people off going down the route of investment.

That does not need to be you. In this book, you will learn about the most common types of investments and will be able to understand how they work and how you could start on your investment journey.

Always consult a financial advisor before you undertake any investment so that you can choose the best one for your circumstances and understand the risks involved.

Wishing you good profits ahead!

# CHAPTER 1

## Why invest?

As mentioned before, you work hard for your money, so it is only fair that you want it to grow as much as it can possibly do.

You might have some short or long-term goals you want to achieve. Having a focus on what you want to achieve will put you in the right direction.

It is essential to understand that if you leave your money sitting in a savings account, then you are not making the most and could be missing real opportunities for growth.

Who wouldn't want to be making more money?

You also want to achieve a healthy financial situation and be able to plan for the future. By investing your money, you can achieve these things a lot quicker.

Understanding how you can grow your money and the tools available for you to do that is the first step you can take towards a healthier financial situation and to achieve your goals.

No investment is risk-free. If you want to have a chance to increase your money, that is something you need to be comfortable with.

There are safer investments than others, with fewer risks, and there are excellent return investments that will ask you to take higher risks. You need to find what you are comfortable with.

Consulting a financial advisor is, therefore, a wise move, as he/she will consider your whole financial situation and will be able to let you know if the investment you are looking to make is the right one for you.

That doesn't mean you should leave the decisions to somebody else. It is your money, after all. It is time for you to start learning and understanding about finance to make the right decisions for yourself.

By all means, consult a financial advisor, learn about successful investors, do your own research, and then you will be able to decide what is best for you.

In terms of investment, you can make your money grow and generate ways to make additional income.

Thinking ahead is also very important. Making retirement plans in advance and investing in them will allow you to be in a much better place when that time comes. You won't have to rely only on your State's Pension, which, most of the time, won't be able to provide you with a sufficient income to live a comfortable life.

You want to ensure you have some money saved for your kids to go to university or to help them climb the property ladder when they grow up.

If something happens to you, having a plan to leave your family in a stable financial situation is also something most people aspire to.

Therefore, investment can profoundly impact many areas of your life and help you grow your money to achieve your goals.

It is a misconception that only wealthy individuals can invest. There are a lot of options open for you too.

Another positive aspect of investing is that you might also indirectly help other people in some instances, so it is not about only you enjoying the benefits.

## The Problem With the Savings Account

The savings account does have an important role, but it is not the only option you have in terms of investment.

You could use it to hold your emergency fund or any money you will need easy access to. It is always advisable to have a minimum of three (but ideally at least six) months of your income saved in case of emergencies.

Having a safety nest will allow you to tackle any emergency without having the added stress to think where to get the money from.

When you invest, sometimes your money will be tied for a while, and you won't be able to access it unless you pay fees, which you should avoid to minimise losses.

The problem with the savings account is the interest rates provided. They are too low, which means any excess money to your emergency fund is not growing as much as it could. There are better investments out there with potentially better returns.

# What is an investment?

It is when you buy something to have some income or profit generated.

Risk and investment go hand-in-hand. If an investment is a low risk, then expect low returns, while the higher the returns, the higher the risks.

# When should you invest?

Ideally, you should think about investing when your debts are paid off.

At a minimum, when your credit debts are all paid off, when you built an emergency fund and when you have some money in your savings account.

Credit debts carry very high interest, and therefore the longer you take to pay them back, the more you owe.

You should also build an emergency fund to cover any emergency that might happen, like a loss of a job or illness. It should contain at least three to six months worth of your monthly income.

When you have money in your savings account above the emergency fund cover, then you are in a financial position to invest.

# How much money do you need to start?

There is no minimum amount to start investing, but it makes sense you start with at least several hundred to make some profit.

Some investments will have a minimum amount, so always check with your financial advisor the optimal amount for your circumstance.

You should also consider how much money you are comfortable investing. There is always a risk factor, and you should only invest what you can potentially afford to lose to be on the safe side.

Never invest money that you can't afford to lose. The key is to build up your savings before you start to invest. That way, you will have the funds to handle something like a job loss or illness.

You shouldn't invest money you need to meet other responsibilities.

## Think long term

When you invest, you hope for greater returns than what you are getting in a savings account, but you have to accept that you need to hold investments for the longer-term. This way, you are giving them the best chance of getting where you want them to be.

Share prices fluctuate, so a longer holding period gives you more chance for good things to happen, to correct the falls from a bad period.

Being a long-term investor rather than a short-term trader means you could benefit from identifying problems and finding solutions. Become more financially savvy.

The longer the holding period, the lower the chance of loss as the minimum average return increases.

# Investing in the stock market will not make you rich overnight.

Investing in the stock market is a slow, steady, and consistent way to build wealth. With a 7% average yearly gain, your initial investment will double in ten years, so it won't happen overnight.

The stock market is one of the greatest wealth-building tools that exist, but you need to follow a few rules.

You need to know what you are investing in, watch the fees, build a diversified portfolio and invest for the long term if you want the best chance to build wealth.

## Do your own research.

You must understand what you are investing in and how it works. You can still use a financial advisor's services, but it is always better to learn the ropes yourself.

If you are interested in investing in a company, in particular, investigate its affairs. You can analyse their financial statements and all other available information about them.

Before making any investment, you should do your own research.

There are publicly available sources of information for almost any industry. The annual report of a company itself gives you a good enough overview of the industry, along with its future growth outlook.

You can also subscribe to trade magazines and websites that cater to a particular industry.

Focus on the company's strengths and weaknesses. Understanding the financial strength of a company is the most crucial step in analysing a stock.

Educate yourself to understand a company's balance sheet, income statement, and cash flow statements.

By understanding more about finance, you will be able to never blindly accept what stock analysts have to say, as you would always be doing your own research too.

## How to stop struggling financially

Get on a budget. It is impossible to manage your money effectively if you have no idea where it is going and how much you need to pay for your bills.

Cut expenses. Identify the areas where you are overspending. If you can reduce spending on nonessentials, you will have more money left over to do more important things, like paying off debt and saving.

Save up an emergency fund. It can help you regain control while keeping out of debt. Emergencies can happen at any time, so ideally, you should save three to six months of living expenses saved.

Stop incurring new debt. Paying off what you owe could free up a considerable amount of cash you can then use for other things.

Earn an extra income. There is no limit to the extra money you can earn. This extra money can be used for debt repayment, savings, or covering the essentials.

# CHAPTER 2

## Types of Investor

What type of investor are you?

- Pre-investor. Someone who is not investing yet.
- Passive investor. Someone who is investing but relies on other people's expertise on how to grow their money. It is the safer option. There is nothing wrong with being a passive investor. At least you are taking steps to succeed financially.
- Active investor. Someone who takes active steps to understand and manage their investment and create their own opportunities to suit their own goals.

## Main Types of investment

These are the main types of investments:

- Shares
- Bonds
- Mutual Funds
- Index Funds
- Investment Funds
- Exchange-Traded Funds (ETFs)
- Certificates of Deposit (CD)
- Property
- Cash
- Options

- Futures
- Annuities
- Retirement
- Assets
- Cryptocurrencies
- Commodities
- Currencies

# CHAPTER 3

## Shares/Stocks/Equities

They are similar terms, but there are some differences.

Stocks is the more generic term. It describes a slice of ownership.

Shares often refer to a portion of ownership of a particular company.

Stocks are divided into shares; a share is the smallest denomination of a company's stock. Each unit of stock is a share in a company.

For example: if a person owns 1% of a company's stocks, you can say they own 1% share in the company.

Equity is for total ownership in the company minus any debt.

Stocks are small units from a company that can be bought and can be sold.

Why do companies offer them? It is a way for them to raise money and find investors.

When you buy a share, you are purchasing a portion of a company and become a shareholder.

As a shareholder, you might have some rights and benefits. For example, you might be able to vote on company matters or even receive dividend payments.

Dividend payment is a share of the profits that a company pay to their shareholders. A company is not obliged to pay dividends. They can be regularly paid or just as a one-off.

Shares do not offer a guarantee of profit, and like all investments, there is a risk. Prices can go up or down.

You can buy shares yourself, or you can pool your money with other people in a collective investment. This is known as a fund.

How long should you invest for? Ideally, several years to allow time to pass if you make a loss due to the market bumps.

If you cannot keep your money away for that long and need access to it sooner, then shares might not be the best option for you at this time.

As the saying goes, do not put all your eggs in one basket. Owning shares in just one company is too risky, and in case the value of a share drops, you lose money.

What are the advantages of shares?

•You might be able to receive dividends
•They can grow in price
•Flexible

What are the disadvantages of shares?

•You might not receive dividends
•Risky

•Market price can fluctuate

As a first-time investor, a safe option for you would be investing in a stocks&shares Isas. An Isa is an individual savings account and stocks & shares Isas allow you to invest in a wide range of shares and funds.

An Isa is Britain's version of what Americans know as the IRA.

You can grow your money in two ways with a share: if the share prices increase, you can make a profit (the value will be higher than when you bought it) and if the company decides to pay dividends to you.

The easiest way for you to buy shares is online from a share dealing platform. You can buy shares from any company listed on the stock exchange.

You should open a trading account. After opening and funding your account, you can buy stocks through the broker's website.

Other options include using a full-service stockbroker or buying stock directly from the company.

How do you pick shares? An excellent place to start is researching companies you already know from your experiences as a customer.

How many shares should you buy? Most people might aim to hold between 10 and 20 stocks.

If you want to buy from the London Stock Exchange or the New York Stock Exchange, you will need a broker. They will also charge you a fee and often work on a commission basis.

How much is a share price? It varies as it depends on the supply and demand from buyers and sellers. If demand is high, so will the cost be.

There are some charges you need to be aware of:

- Account fee. This may be waived depending on the number of trades you make
- Inactivity fee. This could be charged if you do not stick to the minimum number of trades set up for your account. Not many companies are charging this now as they want you to stay with them.
- Buying or selling. You pay a fee each time you buy or sell shares
- Stamp duty. When you buy shares, you usually pay a tax of 0.5% on the transaction. The charge is incurred by the buyer only.

## Dividend Investing

This is a strategy of buying stocks that pay dividends in order to receive income from your investments.

Dividends are payments a corporation makes to shareholders. When you own stocks that pay dividends, you are receiving a share of the company profits.

If the company you own shares of has a dividend reinvestment plan, you can choose to have your dividends reinvested to buy additional shares rather than having them paid out as a profit.

Regular dividend income is a reliable, safe way to grow a nest egg.

In general, companies that pay 60% or less of earnings as dividends are safer bets because they can be predictable.

Look for companies that have a history of stable income and cash flow.

Most income from dividends is taxed as ordinary income, but qualified dividend stocks held for a longer period (60 days or more) are taxed at the lower capital gains tax rates.

# Bonds

This is when you make a loan to a company or the government. They will issue bonds when they need to raise money to finance projects.

The main difference between a bond and a loan is that the bond is tradable. There is usually a market where you can trade them. Loans are agreements between banks and customers and are typically non-tradable.

Bonds offer interest rates. The interest rates can be fixed or variable.

A bond comes with an end date, and when that approaches, all your money must be paid back to you in full.

How much does a bond cost? The market price will depend on:

•The credit quality of who is issuing the bond. The lower the rating, the riskier the bond is. Always check the issuer's background so you can decide if they are worth it or risky.
•The length of time until expiration
•Interest rate

You can sell the bond to other investors. You do not need to stay with it until the end date.

What are the advantages of bonds?

•You get paid interest payments
•You get all the money you invested if you stay with it until the end
•You can resell it at a profit

What are the disadvantages?

•They usually pay lower returns than shares
•Companies can default on the payment to you
•If the interest rate falls, so does your return amount

You might find a bond with a higher interest rate, but that will mean that the higher the interest rate, the higher the default risk.

Avoid investing solely based on the interest rate offered. If the interest rate is high, it means the bonds are riskier, and you have a higher chance of losing all your investment.

When interest rates rise, bonds fall and vice versa. Interest rate risk happens when the rates change from what you were expecting. If the interest rate increases, you will be stuck with a bond returning below the market rates.

The greater the time to reach maturity, the greater the risk you have from interest rates rising.

There are two ways to make money by investing in bonds.

The first is to hold those bonds until their maturity date and collect interest payments on them. Bond interest is usually paid twice a year.

The second way is to sell them at a higher price than what you paid initially.

You can also invest in bond funds, which are when several investors pool money together for a fund manager to buy a large variety of individual bonds.

There are four primary categories of bonds:

- Corporate. They are issued by companies. Unlike shares, bonds issued by companies give you no ownership rights. They are riskier bonds, but they tend to compensate for that by paying higher rates of interest.
- Treasury bonds. Issued by the government. It is a way for politicians to raise money without raising taxes. They can be an excellent option for the low-risk portion of your portfolio.
- Municipal bonds. Issued by cities, states, and counties.
- Agency bonds. Issued by government-affiliated organisations

A bond's price changes daily, where supply and demand determine the price.

When choosing bonds, take into consideration:

- Maturity and duration. Changes in overall interest rates will have more of an effect on bonds with longer maturities. Bonds with longer maturities have, therefore, a greater level of risk due to changes in interest rate, so they offer higher returns (yields) to be more attractive to potential buyers.
- Quality. Some organisations rate the quality of each bond by assigning a credit rating. The better the borrower's credit rating, the lower the yield.

You can lose money on a bond if you sell it before the maturity date for less than you paid or if the issuer defaults on their payments.

The standard interval when you get interest payments from bonds usually is twice a year.

Investing in multiple bonds can provide more frequent monthly payouts as they do not pay at the same time.

It is possible to create a bond portfolio paying monthly income. This can be obtained with the purchase of different bonds (typically six) that will pay you interest on other dates.

Bonds are less likely to lose money than stocks are. So buying some bonds and some stocks can reduce your portfolio's losses.

Bonds can be purchased from several sources, including investment and commercial banks, brokers, and firms.

The minimum investment required to purchase a single bond is about $1,000 though bonds are generally sold in $5,000 increments.

# CHAPTER 4

## Investment Funds

You are not investing alone in a fund. There is a pool of investors who provide money for a collective investment.

It is a safer route than buying shares as you do not have to shoulder the risk all by yourself.

By using a fund, you have a broader selection of investment opportunities, greater management expertise to help you, and lower investment fees than if you were investing on your own.

You do not make individual decisions about how the fund's assets should be invested. You simply choose a fund based on its goals, risk, fees.

A fund manager oversees the fund and decides which securities it should hold, in what quantities, and when the securities should be bought and sold. That is why you benefit from greater management expertise.

You are buying units in this fund. Most funds have a specific theme:

• Geography
• Industry
• Types of investment
• Size of company

There are also different types of funds:

•Mutual funds
•Index funds
•Exchange-traded funds
•Money market funds
•Hedge funds

The advantages of investment funds are:

•They hold different items
•Easy to invest in
•Professional money management is part of the package
•Low cost to purchase

The disadvantages are:

•The fees
•Performance or rate of return is not guaranteed
•You cannot switch your investment as the fund manager has
 control

You should invest for at least five years. If you know you will need access to your money at this time, then perhaps this isn't the right investment for you.

The cheapest route for investing in funds is to use a fund supermarket or platforms. They can be found online.

Investing in funds is a two-stage process. First, you need to pick which platform you want to use; then; then you need to decide what investment to put into it.

You will be charged both for using the platform and buying the funds.

## Mutual Funds

A mutual fund is a type of fund. They are investment strategies that allow you to pool your money together with other investors to purchase a collection of stocks, bonds, and other investments.

One thing to note is that a mutual fund investor does not own the securities in which the fund invests; they only own shares in the fund itself.

All mutual funds allow you to buy or sell your fund shares once a day at the close of the market. The price fluctuates based on the value of the fund's items at the end of each business day.

You can make money in three possible ways:

• Income earned from dividends on shares
• Interest on bonds
• An increase in the price of securities. If the fund share price increases, you can then sell your shares for a profit.

There are four types of mutual funds:

• Those that invest in share (equity funds). They buy shares of a collection of publicly-traded companies; therefore, they invest in corporate shares. They have a higher potential for growth, but they experience price fluctuations.
• Bonds (fixed-income funds). The most common type of fixed income mutual funds. Investors are paid a fixed amount back on

their initial investment. Bonds funds invest in government and corporate debt. They are considered a safer investment than shares but have less potential for growth than equity funds.These funds are often actively managed and seek to buy relatively undervalued bonds to sell them at a profit.

•Money market (short-term debt). It consists of safe short-term debt instruments, mostly government Treasury bills. This is a safe place to park your money. You won't get substantial returns, but you won't have to worry about losing your initial investment. A typical return is a little more than the amount you would earn in a regular checking or savings account.

•Both stocks and bonds.The objective is to reduce the risk by diversifying.

•Income fund. They provide current income on a steady basis. These funds invest primarily in government and high-quality corporate debt, holding these bonds until maturity provides interest payments. They are therefore more long-term. They may appreciate, but their primary objective is to provide steady cash flow to investors. Typical investors are conservative and retirees. Because they produce regular income, tax-conscious investors may want to avoid these funds.

Every mutual fund is designed to spread around risk while capturing market gains.

The advantages of mutual funds:

•You get the benefit of having a professional manager reviewing the portfolio on an ongoing basis
•The cost of trading is spread over all investors in the fund, lowering the cost per individual
•Mutual funds also invest in a variety of different sectors, diversifying the portfolio instantly

The disadvantages are:

- High fees
- Tax inefficiency
- Poor trade execution
- Potential for management abuses

Mutual funds can be purchased directly from a mutual fund company, a bank, or a brokerage firm. Before you start investing, you will need to have an account.

There are a variety of fees that may be associated with mutual funds.

Some funds come with transaction charges for buying and selling or commissions.

Annual fund operating fees are a yearly percentage of the funds under management.

Some funds charge a redemption fee if you sell shares you've only owned for a short time.

Like in all investments, there are risks too. There is always the possibility that the value of your mutual fund will depreciate.

Mutual funds are typically better suited for long-term investors.

If you think you will need your money soon, then a mutual fund may not be the best option. This is because the return in that amount of time (once removing the cost of the fees) may not be enough to make the investment worth it.

# Index Funds

An index fund is an investment that tracks a market index (ex. S&P 500- the top 500 stocks in the USA).

They are typically made up of stocks or bonds. There are an index and an index fund for nearly every financial market in existence.

The fund manager builds a portfolio whose holdings mirror the securities of a particular index.

It tries to mimic the composition and performance of a financial market index. It aims to match rather than exceed its performance.

It is a type of mutual fund or exchange-traded fund (ETF).

To invest:

- Pick the index. There are hundreds of different indexes you can track using index funds. You can also find sector indexes tied to specific industries, country indexes that target stocks in single nations, and style indexes that emphasise fast-growing companies.
- Choose a fund
- Buy shares

The advantages are:

- Broad market exposure. Index funds are available for a wide variety of investments. You can buy stock index funds and bond index funds.
- Low operating expenses. They have a lower management expense ratio. The manager of index funds trades holdings less often, incurring fewer transaction fees and commissions.
- Low portfolio turnover.
- You can invest with less risk. Most indexes include dozens or even hundreds of stocks and other investments, and the diversification leaves you less likely to suffer significant losses.
- As they follow a passive investment strategy, they have lower expenses and fees than actively managed funds. The index fund manager has to buy the stocks or other investments in an index. He does not have to pick and choose individual performing stocks.
- You will pay less in taxes. They are quite tax-efficient compared with many other investments.

The disadvantages of an index fund investment are:

- You will never beat the market. They are designed to match the market's performance.
- You don't have any loss protection. Index funds track their markets in good times and bad, and when the market plunges, your index fund will plunge as well.
- You won't always own the stocks you like
- No control over holdings

The investment tends to be over the long term to lead to positive performance.

Investors make an initial minimum investment ($3,000 -$10,000) and pay annual costs to maintain the fund (a small percentage of your cash invested).

You can purchase an index fund directly from a mutual fund company or a brokerage. To buy shares in your chosen index fund, you can open an account directly with the mutual fund company that offers the fund.

## Exchange-traded funds (ETFs)

It is a bundle of investments that are sold on an exchange. Like individual stocks, ETFs shares are traded throughout the day at prices that change based on supply and demand.

The fund provider owns the assets, designs a fund to track their performance, and then sells the shares in that fund to investors.

Shareholders own a portion of an ETF, but they don't own the fund's underlying assets.

The main difference with mutual funds is that ETFs shares trade throughout the day just like ordinary stocks, whereas mutual funds only trade once a day after the market closes.

ETFs have become prevalent investments. They are ideal for beginner investors due to their many benefits such as low expense ratios, liquidity, range of investment, and low investment threshold.

Types of ETFs:

• Bond. It might include government bonds, corporate bonds, municipal bonds. Bond ETFs are not like individual online bonds as they don't have a maturity date, so the most common use for them is to generate regular cash payments to the investor. These payments come from the interest generated by the individual bonds within the fund.
• Industry. Track a particular industry
• Commodity. Invest in things like crude oil or gold
• Currency. Invest in foreign currencies

An exchange-traded fund has a price that allows it to be easily bought and sold.

You can have an actively-managed ETF where portfolio managers are more involved in buying and selling shares of companies; however, a more actively managed fund will have a higher expense fee than passively managed ETFs.

Advantages of ETFs:

• They provide investors with the ability to gain as stock prices rise and fall
• Investors can benefit from companies that pay dividends
• ETFs shareholders are entitled to a proportion of the profits
• Flexible. ETFs are bought and sold during the day when the markets are open
• They provide portfolio diversification
• Lower cost. They are passively managed, having much lower expense ratios if compared to actively managed funds
• Tax benefits. Due to structural differences, mutual funds incur more capital taxes than ETFs. They have lower capital gains and they are payable only upon the sale of the ETF.

Disadvantages of ETFs:

- Subject to market fluctuation
- Subject to management fees and other expenses
- The cost could be higher. If you compare ETFs with investing in a specific stock, prices are higher.

ETFs trade through online brokers and traditional broker-dealers. You will need to open a brokerage account.

## Money Market Funds

It is a kind of mutual fund that invests in highly solvent, short instruments. They are intended to offer investors high solvency with a very low level of risk.

A money market fund is an investment that is sponsored by an investment fund company.

A money market fund generates income but little capital appreciation, which means a small rise to the initial investment.

Money market accounts are a good investment if you can maintain a high minimum balance, limit your withdrawal and understand that you are not protected against inflation.

They are classified into various types:

- Prime money fund. Invests in floating rate debt and commercial paper of non-treasury assets
- Government money fund. Invests at least 99.5% of its total assets in cash, government securities
- Treasury fund. Invest in standard US treasury issued debt securities

- Tax-exempt money fund. Offer earnings that are free from US tax

Advantages of money market funds:

- Great place to park money for the short term. Less risky because these types of funds invest in low-risk vehicles. Often generates a low single-digit return for investors.
- They invest in highly liquid securities. This means investors can buy and sell them with ease.

The disadvantages are:

- Purchasing power can suffer. They can generate returns below inflation, which means you lose purchasing power.
- Fees can eat up a substantial chunk of the profit. They often need a minimum balance to avoid a monthly service charge.
- They are not government-insured. If the investment fund company goes bust, you might lose all your money.
- Low-interest rate
- Inflation risk

You generally must pay tax on the interest you receive or on dividends paid by those funds as you earn them. Unless they are held in a tax-deferred retirement account.

Unlike CDs, you can close a money-market account at any time without incurring a penalty.

You can buy money market funds from an investment fund company, brokerage firms, and banks.

# Hedge Funds

A hedge fund is a pooled investment fund that trades in relatively liquid assets and can make extensive use of more complex trading to improve performance.

A hedge fund typically pays its investment manager a management fee and a performance fee.

Investors in hedge funds are required to be qualified (well-off) investors who are assumed to be aware of the investment risks and accept them because of the potential returns.

The main goals of a hedge fund are to maximise returns and minimise risk. They aim to try to make money despite the market fluctuating up or down.

They are almost always only available to accredited investors. To be considered an accredited investor, you must qualify by one of the following:

• Have a personal income of $200,000 or more for yourself only.
• You must have a personal net worth of over $1 million.
• Must be a higher-up (executive, director) involved in the hedge fund or have an employee benefit plan or trust fund worth at least $5 million


Most hedge funds operate on a 2 and 20 manager compensation scheme, which gives the hedge fund manager 2% of the assets and an incentive fee of 20%.

Types:

- Macro. Invest in stocks, bonds, futures, options, and sometimes currencies
- Equity. Attempts to hedge against declines in equity markets by investing in stocks or stock indices and later selling them
- Relative value arbitrage hedge funds. Buy securities that are expected to appreciate while simultaneously selling the ones that are likely to depreciate.
- Distressed hedge funds. They are frequently involved in loan payouts or restructuring.

Hedge funds invest in land, real estate, currencies, derivatives, and others. In short, they can invest in anything.

Advantages of a hedge fund:

- Flexibility. People do not trade hedge funds publicly; therefore, they are more flexible as there is no particular body regulating their performance.
- Aggressive investment strategy. This is important to achieve a higher return.
- Increases the chance of diversification. The fund can add diversification and also reduce risk.
- Expert advice and transparency. The hedge fund managers are also well versed in financial management matters.

The disadvantages of hedge funds are:

- Hedge fund fees. They have a fee structure known as 2 and 20. Investors pay a 2% in management fee for the operations of the

fund. Additionally, they also pay 20% to the fund manager as a performance fee for any profits made through the year.
- Risks and returns. They are regarded as taking too many risks.
- They are not as liquid as stocks or bonds
- May only allow you to withdraw your money after you've been invested for a certain amount of time or during set times of the year.

Minimum initial investment amounts for hedge funds range from $100,000 to over $2 million.

It is extremely difficult for individual investors to gain access to a quality hedge fund, but you could find an indirect method of investing in one. You could invest in the stock of a financial company that operates hedge funds.

# CHAPTER 5

## Property

Property investment is when you buy a property to generate some income.

You can benefit from regular income from rental and from selling the property in the future (hoping its value has increased with time).

With low-interest rates, volatility in the market, and rents still likely to increase, property is ideal for providing income and capital growth.

You might have to consider:

• Where you are going to invest
• Type of property you want to purchase. You will need to decide what type of rental you are looking for. It helps to have a target tenant in mind. You can have single lets, which are the regular type of rent to an individual or a family, or HMOs which is a house share where you rent room by room to unrelated people.
• Taxes due


You can buy to sell or buy to let.

If you want to purchase a buy to let investment property, you can either pay the price in full or with a buy to let mortgage. This will largely depend on the type of property you want to invest in and the property investment company you use.

The good news is that real estate consistently increases in value over time and can return more than other investments.

Property is not vulnerable to fluctuations in the stock market, and there can also be tax benefits.

Like with all investments, there are costs to take into consideration:

- Mortgage repayments. This will be one of your most significant expenses.
- Property management fees. Having your property managed professionally comes at a cost. A property manager is someone who will manage the property monthly. Most commonly, they will charge you a percentage of the monthly rent. Their responsibilities will be: managing the rent, tenants, maintenance and repairs, property records and accounting, and taxes. You don't have to hire one, but you should consider their expertise as a reason to do it.
- Insurance. Landlord protection insurance, income protection insurance, and life insurance are just a few examples of types of policies that you will need to consider.
- Maintenance costs. Some people put aside 1% of the purchased price for ongoing maintenance costs.
- Strata fees/service charges. Apartment owners pay service charges for the upkeep of communal areas and shared services. Typically these are paid by the landlord and not the tenant. The more features the complex boasts, the higher strata fees will typically be.
- Solicitor fees
- Land Registry fees
- Surveys
- Stamp Duty

- Estate agency fees
- Surveys

You will also need to have enough money for a deposit.

You can invest in property via:

- REITs. Real Estate Investment Trusts. They are investment funds that solely invest in property. They are easier to invest and easier to get out of because they are a pooled fund. This means several investors buy property, which the fund then owns. They have a low entry point. Many property funds invest in commercial property. Returns are higher than those available from the residential market.
- Buy to Let. You buy and then let out. You are renting out your property to tenants who will pay your mortgage for you and also provide some extra income. You aim to make money in two ways: the monthly rental income and the growth in the property's value over time. There is no guarantee that your property will be occupied all the time, and when it is empty, you will need to make the mortgage payments from your own pocket. You are responsible for maintaining the property.
- Property Development. You can make good and quick returns by buying cheap property to develop. You can cut development costs by doing the work yourself. Property values can be disproportionately increased by spending on repairs and improvements. It takes time to develop property, so the market may have fallen by the time you come to sell. You will need to manage the development yourself or pay someone else to do it. You need to work to strict budgets to make a profit. It can take a long time to sell a property, and you will still have to pay the mortgage.

- Buy a new build to sell on. It can be risky as you haven't seen the finished property. The developer can go bust. You can also run into problems selling the property. The benefit is that you can often get a good deal. You might be able to sell the property for a profit. You can add value to the property by decorating or furnishing it.
- Invest in property abroad

This is a long-term investment.

The advantages of investing in property:

- You can earn rental income
- You can benefit from capital growth if the property increases in value
- Interest on an investment home loan is tax-deductible
- Property investment can be less volatile than shares

The disadvantages are:

- Time-consuming
- Not a liquid asset, so you will not turn it into cash quickly in an emergency
- Dealing with rental tenants and maintenance issues
- Vulnerability to damage

If you want to purchase a property investment, you should consider:

- Paying down personal debt
- Securing a downpayment. Investment properties generally require a larger downpayment than a personal one. You will

need at least a 20% downpayment, given that mortgage insurance isn't available on rental properties.
•Find the right location
•Invest in Landlord Insurance. In addition to homeowner insurance

## Real Estate Investment Secrets

Some of the fundamentals you should consider are immigration to the area, population increase, transportation improvements, schools nearby, vacancy rates, job growth, industries near the area.

If you buy in those areas, you will do well in the longer term.

Be open to partnering with other investors and deals. When you have partners, you can take advantage of opportunities that you wouldn't be able to on your own.

With partners, you can focus on the pieces of the deal that match your skillset or goals.

You may want to do some research on successful investors in real estate. They have the experience and knowledge in this sector.

Consider all the possibilities for making money as a real estate investor. You can invest in rental properties, flip homes in disrepair, and buy and sell commercial properties.

Experienced real estate investors explore all the options and do not limit themselves to just one income stream.

Diversifying is an excellent way to increase potential profits as well as spread the risk.

You must have a good sense of the market and understand the process of valuing properties. Analyze the properties without getting emotionally invested. Be detached and analytical so that you can make sound decisions.

## Options

It is a contract that allows an investor to buy or sell an instrument over a certain period of time.

You have the right to exercise that option at any point up until the expiration date. It is an option; therefore, you do not have to exercise it if you don't want to.

Options belong to the larger groups of securities known as derivatives. A derivative is called that way because its price is dependent on or derived from the price of something else.

Note that options are not the same as stocks because they do not represent ownership of a company.

You can withdraw or walk away from an options contract at any point.

The price of the option is a percentage of the underlying asset or security.

It is essentially all about determining the probabilities of future price events.

Types of options:

- Call Option. It is a contract that gives the investor the right to buy a certain amount of shares of a particular security or commodity at a specified price over a certain amount of time. In this case, you want the stock to go up in price so that you can make a profit off of your contract by exercising your right to buy those stocks and usually immediately sell them to cash in on the profit.
- Put Options. It is a contract that gives the investor the right to sell a certain amount of shares of a particular security or commodity at a specified price over a certain amount of time. In this case, you want the security to drop in price to make a profit or sell the put option if you think the price will go up.

Options are also known to be:
- American options. Your option can be exercised at any time between the date of purchase and the expiration date. Because the right to exercise early has some value, an American option typically carries a higher premium than a European option.
- European options. They can only be exercised at the end of their lives on their expiration date.

In both call-out or put options, you can exercise your right to sell or buy up until the expiration date of your contract. The more time left on the contract, the higher the premiums are going to be.

When the contract expires, you can renew it. This could be weekly, monthly or quarterly.

The advantages of options are:
- They are cost-efficient
- They have a high return potential
- Lower risk

The disadvantages are:
- Less Liquidity
- High commissions
- Time decay. The value of your option premium decreases by some percentages each day.

You can only buy or sell options through a brokerage. You would also have to pay the fee (premium) to get the contract.

First, choose the stock that you wish to use as your underlying asset. Then you need to decide if you think the stock price will rise or fall.

## Futures

They are financial derivative contracts that obligate the parties to buy or sell an asset at a predetermined future date and price.

The buyer must purchase, or the seller must sell the asset at the set price, regardless of the current market price at the expiration date. The traders lock in the price of the asset.

A futures contract allows an investor to speculate on the direction of a security, commodity, or financial instrument.

Futures are derivatives because their value is based on an underlying asset.

Types of futures contract:
• Commodity futures. Ex: crude oil, natural gas, corn, and wheat
• Stock index futures
• Currency futures
• Precious metal futures. Gold and silver
• US treasury futures for bonds and other products

What is the difference between options and futures? In options, the contracts give the holder the right to buy or sell the assets any time before the expiration date. In a futures contract, the buyer is obligated to take possession of the commodity at the expiration time.

As in options, the buyer of a futures contract can sell their position at any time before expiration and be free of their obligation.

The investor does not need to put up 100% of the contract's value amount when entering the trade. The broker would require an initial amount, a fraction of the total contract value.

If a trader bought a futures contract and the price of the commodity rose and was trading above the original contract price, then they would have a profit.

Speculators can also take sell if they predict the price of the asset will fall.

Advantages of futures:

- Easy pricing
- High Liquidity

Disadvantages of futures:
- No control over future events
- Price fluctuations
- Potential reduction in asset price as the expiration date approaches

Investing in futures requires a broker. Many future markets trade beyond regular market hours.

Commissions on future trades are very low and are charged when the position is closed.

# CHAPTER 6

## Cash

It is the safer type of investment as it is less risky, but it offers a low return rate.

It is usually short-term, generally fewer than 90 days, and provides a return in interest payments.

Some of the best cash investments are CDs, government bond funds, short-term corporate funds, S&P 500 index funds, dividend stock funds, municipal bond funds.

Types of cash investments:

- Savings account. The interest rate on these accounts is minimal.
- Money market. Collective investment schemes that invest your money in cash or equivalents of cash at very short-term having a maturity period of fewer than six months. Interest rates will be higher the longer the deposit is for. You can earn a higher interest on those rather than on high-interest savings accounts. The interest you earn is fixed and does not fluctuate, and you can choose how long you want to invest. One negative aspect is the lack of access you will have to your cash during the fixed term. You will be able to withdraw earlier but at a cost, which could be interest rate plus a fee. Another negative aspect is the agreed interest rate. If the interest rate gets higher during the agreed period, that will not reflect on your term deposit as yours had a fixed interest deal.
- Certificate of deposit (CD). You agree to leave a lump sum deposit untouched for a fixed period and in return, the bank will offer you an interest rate premium. They are also known as CDs. If you withdraw earlier, there will be penalties and they can vary depending on the bank. In order not to lose money, ensure you do not make an earlier withdrawal.
- Money in term deposits. Fixed interest rate in exchange for depositing it for an agreed time.
- Cash Isas. Cash or shares Isa. The main benefit of an Isa is that you earn interest on your savings, without paying tax on the earnings (up until a certain amount, in the UK currently that amount is £20,000). You can top up the amount annually, but you can only open one Cash ISA per year. It is possible to transfer to another Cash Isa with another provider though. The Isa allowance is for both cash and shares Isa, so the £20,000 limit can be divided between these two investments. Some providers can offer a flexible Isa, which means you can

withdraw and replace money provided you do that within the same tax year. Check with your provider if they can offer this service.

An Isa is Britain's version of what Americans know as the IRA.

The advantages of a cash investment:
•If investing in a bank account, they are insured
• You have certainty of future funds

The disadvantages of cash investment:
•Low returns
•Account fees. Sometimes these fees can exceed the interest rate on your account and eat away at your investment.

You can open a cash investment account online, over the phone, or at your local bank.

## Certificate of Deposit (CD)

A certificate of deposit (CD) is similar to a savings account that holds a fixed amount of money for a fixed period, and in exchange, the issuing bank pays interest. It is considered to be one of the safest savings options.

At the end of the fixed time, you get your original money plus the interest rate. You agree not to make any withdrawals for a certain period. If you withdraw funds early, you will have to pay an early withdrawal penalty.

Longer CDs term lengths can be more attractive than shorter term lengths.

When you hold a CD, the bank will apply interest to your account at regular intervals. This is usually done either monthly or quarterly.

Types of CDs:

- Bump-up CDs. You don't get stuck with a low return if interest rates rise after you buy one. You get to keep your existing CD account and switch to the new, higher rate. You might have to inform your bank in advance that you want to exercise your bump-up option. This type of CD often starts paying out lower interest rates than standard CDs.
- Step-up CDs.They come with regularly scheduled interest rate increases. Increases might come every six or seven months.
- Brokered CDs
- Jumbo CDs.Very high minimum balance requirements.
- Liquid or no-penalty CDs. Allow you to withdraw your funds early without paying a penalty. This enables you to move your funds to a higher paying CD if the opportunity arises, but it comes at a price. They may pay lower interest rates.

Let your bank know before the renewal deadline if you want to do something other than roll your money into a new CD (auto-renew).

When the term finishes, you have the following options:

- You can transfer the funds to your checking or savings account.
- You can switch to a different CD with a longer or shorter term.

If you are interested in using CDs as a key part of your savings plan, you might consider a ladder.

A ladder is a process that involves first buying several CDs with different terms so they will mature at regular intervals and then reinvest the money into longer-term CDs as the initial ones mature.

Ladders help you avoid locking up all your money in a low-paying CD, and they help you avoid cashing out early and paying penalties.

CDs are not a liquid investment because you can't withdraw your cash early without paying penalties and fees. Anyone with liquidity needs would be a poor candidate for long-term CDs.

Advantages of CDs:

• Flexible terms. If you don't want to be tied up for a long time, you can easily opt for a shorter period.
• Safety
• Better return than a savings account
• Wide selection
• Fixed, predictable return


Disadvantages of CDs:

• Limited liquidity. You can't access your money as quickly as a traditional savings account. If you withdraw money before the end of the term, you will have to pay a penalty.
• Inflation risk. CDs rate may be lower than inflation, which means your money may lose its purchasing power over time.

When opening a CD, you should pay attention to the CD term length, the interest rate, minimum deposit requirement, and early withdrawal penalty fee.

Ensure you check out the issuer's background or deposit broker to ensure that the CD is from a reputable institution.

Most CDs are purchased directly from banks; many brokerage firms and independent salespeople also offer them.

Opening a CD is very similar to opening any standards bank deposit account.

Each bank and credit union establishes a minimum deposit required to open each CD.

## Currencies

Investing in foreign currency can be a great way to diversify your portfolio, and it is exceptionally popular.

Investing in currency involves buying the currency of one country while selling that of another. This is done through the foreign exchange market or forex.

There are three ways you can trade foreign currency:

- Spot trading. Currency pairs are exchanged when the trade is settled, which means instant trading.
- Forward trading. You agree to buy or sell foreign currency at a set price on a set date in the future. The price will be settled and you will be insulated from volatility when it's time to trade.
- Future trading. On a future trading contract, you are legally bound to make the trade.

While forex can be lucrative, there may be more ups and downs than the stock market. The forex market can be highly profitable, with the potential to multiply your initial investment overnight.

Both short-term and long-term trading of foreign currency can be profitable.

Consider talking to a financial advisor about investing in currency and whether it's a good fit for your portfolio.

The foreign exchange market (forex) is a market where world currencies are traded 24 hours a day. Traders bet on the movements of currencies relative to each other.

The forex market operates between individuals represented by brokers, between brokers and banks, and between banks.

Advantages of investing in currencies:

• Large and global market
• Good for beginners
• 24 hours a day
• Low transaction costs
• High Liquidity
• Low capital requirements


Disadvantages of investing in currencies:

• Lack of transparency
• Complex price determination process
• High risk
• High volatility

You don't need much capital to get started: $500 to $1,000 is usually enough.

You can open an account with a forex broker and trade currencies from around the world.

# CHAPTER 7

## Annuities

It is a type of retirement income that you can buy with your pension pot. It is a contract between you and an insurance company.

It pays a regular retirement income either for life or for a set period. An annuity should be used as a  way to supplement your income in retirement.

The insurance company will invest your money. The most common way to invest is through mutual funds. From these earnings, the insurance company will make regular payments to you.

Annuity payments are taxed as ordinary income, which is a higher rate than if you were charged for capital gains from other retirement investment accounts.

They include:

- Lifetime annuities. It pays you an income for life and when you die, it will pay a nominated beneficiary.
- Fixed-term annuities. It pays you an income for a set period (usually five to ten years) and a maturity amount at the end. You can then purchase another retirement income product or just take the cash. It guarantees a minimum rate of interest on your money as well as a fixed number of payments from the insurance company.

- Variable annuity. It allows you to invest your money in different securities. The payments you receive will depend on how well your investments perform.
- Indexed annuity.  It combines the benefits of both fixed and variable products. The returns you earn from an index annuity aren't based on the investment decisions you make. Instead, your money will follow the performance of a stock market index.

You can only use a quarter of your pension pot to buy an annuity as tax-free cash, and the income you receive is taxed as normal income.

How much retirement income you can get will depend on:
- Your health
- How big your pension pot is
- The annuities rate at the time you buy
- Where you expect to live when you retire
- How old you are when you buy
- Which annuity type, income options, and features you choose

You need to think carefully because once you buy an annuity, you can't change your mind.

An annuity is just one of several options you have for using your pension pot to provide a retirement income, so consider all your options carefully.

If you have a medical condition, are overweight, or smoke, you might be able to get a higher income through an enhanced annuity.

Some of the medical conditions that entitle you to get this type of cover are stroke, cancer, diabetes, heart attack, kidney failure, chronic asthma, multiple sclerosis, and high blood pressure.

Always compare companies to see what you can get. When doing so, ensure you disclose any medical conditions and lifestyle issues to get an accurate figure.

You can choose between:
- An immediate annuity. You begin receiving payouts straight away.
- Deferred one. You can pay a lump sum or a series of payments into it, but you won't receive a payout until later. This will allow your money to earn interest. You can put money towards your annuity and you won't have to pay tax on it until you start receiving payments. This can give a chance for your money to grow.

Annuities can get very expensive. Any time you consider an annuity contract, you need to understand all the fees that come with it to be sure that you pick the best annuity for your personal goals and situation.

The advantages of annuities are:
- Tax-deferred growth. You pay no income taxes on the earnings from your annuity investments until you make withdrawals or start receiving payments.
- You can make unlimited contributions
- Choice of investment options
- There are no mandatory withdrawals
- Death benefit

• Lifetime income benefit

The disadvantages of choosing an annuity are:

• Low returns
• Tax disadvantages. Payments are taxed as ordinary income.
• Penalties for early withdrawal
• High commissions

You should also be aware of the fees:
• Variable annuities have administrative fees, as well as mortality and expense fees. Insurance companies charge these, which often run about 1.25% of your account's value, to cover the costs and risks of insuring your money.
• Surrender charges are common. This is when you make more withdrawals than you are entitled to. The insurance company could limit withdrawals. The fees are often high.
• Another fee to consider is the investment management fees, which will depend on how you invest with a variable annuity.
• Some annuities will have additional riders (optional guarantees) that will come at a fee. One example is the enhanced death benefit. A rider can cost up to 50% of the value of your account.

You buy annuities from insurance companies.

Remember, always shop around and consult a financial advisor. This is not your only option.

# Retirement

Retirement can last for 30 years or more, depending on when you retire and how long you live.

Most people have more than one source of income in retirement. This is quite important as what you will get from a State Pension will not be enough in most cases.

To determine how much you will need for your retirement, you need to draw up a budget of how much you are likely to spend.

Beware that your pension income is taxable, just like any other income.

Why would you invest in your retirement? If you are looking forward to having a comfortable retirement, you have to think about investing in it; otherwise, it won't happen.

As you are considering investing in your retirement, a good balance between risk and investment is the key.

These are some of the things you could do:

- Construct a total return portfolio. A portfolio of stocks and bonds index funds. It is designed to achieve a respectable long-term rate of return. You can withdraw a percentage a year. You are targeting the long term (10 to 20 years). You must maintain a diversified allocation. You can work with a financial advisor to help you create one.

- Retirement income funds. It is a specialised type of mutual fund. Your money is automatically allocated across a diversified portfolio of stocks and bonds. The investments are managed to produce monthly income, which is distributed to you. With this type of investment, you retain control of your money and can access it at any time. Note that if you withdraw some of your principal, your future monthly income will subsequently go down.

An alternative option for building a retirement pot is to open an Isa.

A lifetime ISA is a type of ISA that lets you build up a long-term fund. You won't be able to take money out of the account until you reach 60 years old, not without paying a 25% charge.

An Isa is Britain's version of what Americans know as the IRA.

Advantages of retirement investment:
- Not only relying on State Pension
- More comfortable and happier retirement
- Not having to be a burden on your family

There are no disadvantages in planning for your retirement. You only have to gain.

# Chapter 8

## Cryptocurrencies

Think of them as digital assets, digital money. A crypto is a digital currency that can be used to buy goods and services. They work using a technology called the blockchain.

Blockchain is a decentralised technology spread across many computers that manage and record transactions. They are not issued by a bank and are unregulated.

Every time you buy a crypto, the transaction is stored in a ledger in the form of a computerised database.

The database, through a process of cryptography, secures transaction records, controls the creation of additional coins, and verify the transfer of coin ownership.

Bitcoin, first released in 2009, is the first decentralised cryptocurrency. Other cryptocurrencies have been since created.

Ownership of cryptocurrency units can be proved exclusively cryptographically.

Tokens, cryptocurrencies, and other types of digital assets that are not bitcoin are collectively known as alternative cryptocurrencies or altcoins.

Altcoins often have underlying differences with bitcoin. Ethereum is the most actively used blockchain globally and has the most considerable following of any altcoins.

A blockchain is a continuously growing list of records, called blocks linked and secured using cryptography.

By design, blockchains are resistant to modification of the data.   A blockchain provides the validity of each cryptocurrency's coins.

Most cryptocurrencies are designed to gradually decrease the production of that currency, placing a cap on the total amount of that currency that will ever be in circulation.

The cryptocurrency within a wallet is not tied to people but instead to one or more specific keys.

Bitcoin owners are not identifiable, but all transactions are publicly available in the blockchain.

Cryptocurrencies are used primarily outside existing banking and governmental institutions and are exchanged over the internet.

Cryptocurrency exchanges allow a customer to trade cryptocurrencies for other assets, such as conventional flat money, or trade between different digital currencies.

There are ATMs for cryptos already in use and more being developed. You can use a card similar to a debit/credit card to withdraw money and pay for things you buy (not widely available yet).

Cryptocurrency networks display a lack of regulation that has been criticised as enabling criminals who seek to evade taxes and launder money.

Transactions that occur through the use and exchange of these altcoins are independent of formal banking systems and can make tax evasion simpler.

Some of the top Cryptocurrencies are:

- Bitcoin. The most known crypto. Invented in 2008 and in use since 2009.
- Ethereum. Also known as ETH. It has a decentralised software platform that enables applications to be built and run. The goal behind Ethereum is to create a decentralised suite of financial products that anyone in the world can have free access to regardless of nationality, ethnicity, or faith. Ethereum is a software platform based on blockchain technology in which users can exchange a cryptocurrency called ether. It is currently the second-largest digital currency after Bitcoin.
- Litecoin. Also known as LTC. It has a faster block generation rate than Bitcoin and hence offers a faster transaction confirmation time. There are a growing number of merchants who accept Litecoin.
- Cardano. Also known as ADA. Still in its early stages. It aims to be the financial operating system of the world by establishing decentralised financial products.

- Bitcoin Cash. Also known as BCH. It can process transactions more quickly than the Bitcoin network. Waiting times are shorter and processing fees lower.
- Stellar. Also, know and XLM. Designed to connect financial institutions for large transactions. Huge transactions between banks and investment firms that typically would take several days and cost a lot of money can now be done nearly instantaneously with no intermediaries and cost little to nothing for those making the transaction. It is still an open blockchain that anyone can use. The system allows for cross-border transactions between any currencies. The network requires users to hold Lumens to be able to transact on the network.
- Binance Coin. Also known as BNB. It is a platform where users can buy and sell finance coins and use BNB to convert other cryptocurrencies from one to another.
- Tether. Also known as USDT. Part of a group of stable coins aims to peg their market value to a currency or other external reference point to reduce volatility.
- It attempts to smooth out price fluctuations to attract users who may otherwise be cautious. Tether's price is tied directly to the price of the US dollar.
- Monero. Also known as XMR. It is a secure, private and untraceable currency.

Do your research before adding cryptos to your portfolio. Cryptos are risky.

Investing in cryptocurrencies is very speculative. This market is extremely volatile, and there's a real possibility of significant losses.

Advantages of cryptos:
- Cryptos offer speedy, low-cost money transfers. This makes using them for international money transfers popular.
- Cryptos are free from authorities and can't be frozen
- Some people consider them to be the currency of the future.
- Some supporters like the fact that cryptocurrency removes central banks from managing the money supply since over time these banks tend to reduce the value of money via inflation.
- Cryptocurrencies are global, meaning they have the same value in every country
- Cryptocurrencies are exchanged from person to person on the web without a middleman
- Bitcoin transactions are completely anonymous and private
- Low, minimal fees
- Fast
- Non-inflationary
- Payment freedom
- Central governments can't take it away

Disadvantages of cryptos:
- The future of cryptocurrency is not guaranteed. Investors who want to speculate in this market should probably stick with the most well-known names, such as bitcoin, ethereal, and litecoin.
- Since cryptocurrencies are virtual and lack a central storehouse, an account balance can be wiped out. If a user loses the private key to their wallet, the cryptocurrency they own is unrecoverable.
- Scammers can also hijack someone's mobile account by impersonating an account holder.
- Very speculative
- Many people are still unaware of cryptos
- Possible government interference. They can be banned.

• Lack of recourse
• Used in money laundering/black market

To buy cryptocurrencies you will need a wallet, an online app that can hold your currency.

You create an account on an exchange, and then you can transfer real money to buy cryptocurrencies.

Only use a wallet from a well-established firm. Do your research.

Coinbase and Binance are two of the world's largest bitcoin trading platforms.

If you want to buy bitcoin and other cryptos and sell them again, there will be several fees such as transaction fees, deposit fees, withdrawal fees, trading fees.

# CHAPTER 9

## Alternative Investment Opportunities

You might hold some assets that can provide you with income either through sales or asset growth over time.

Some of them can be a one-off opportunity, and some of them can be transformed into a source of permanent income.

This could be achieved because they grow in value as time goes by, they are rare, or because you might have found a buyer who can offer you a substantial amount of money for what you hold.

They might be assets you can sell at a profit or assets you might want to hold for long as they will grow in value over time.

Let's look at the most common types.

## Antiques and Collectibles

Antiques and collectibles have a higher return on investment as they aren't influenced by inflation rates or the stock market.

The value of antiques and collectibles do not fluctuate; they only rise with the rarity and quality of the good.

They can offer impressive returns over the longer term. You should seek specialists' advice or develop a broad knowledge.

Some of the best antiques and collectibles for investment include clocks, coins, cameras, comic books, stamps, whiskey, board games.

One of the world's most valuable antiques is a Pinner Qing Dynasty vase worth $80.2 million, according to sammydvintage.com.

The first step in identifying and valuing antiques and collectibles is often determining the item's maker by researching a mark or signature.

When identifying antique furniture, one of the first things to look at is the sale or period.

The less that was done to the original item to alter it, the more it is worth.

If you want to get antiques valued, a really good place to go is antique auctions, as they have specialist valuers, and if you take the item or send photos, they will usually give you a free valuation in the hope that you will see your goods through them.

The difference between antique and vintage is the age. Antique items must be at least 100 years old.

Advantages are:
• You can collect anything for investment purposes
• The rarest items appreciate over the longer term

- They are tangible
- They can be portable
- Global investments
- Gain capital value above the average rate of inflation
- You can enjoy your investment
- High-quality products
- Stylish

Disadvantages:
- The antique market is not regulated
- If you need to recoup the cash tied up in your investment, there is no guarantee they will sell at the prices you want.
- They can be extremely expensive
- Volatile industry
- Expensive to keep, maintain and store

You can find antiques and collectibles online, in stores, and also in auctions.

You can sell them online.

# Cars

Can you make money from cars? When you think about this type of investment, you probably think about the classic car market or vintage vehicles.

You can also find ways to make money from your car by renting it out for special occasions like weddings.

Many people consider a car an investment because of the large price tag; however, investments make you money. A vehicle depreciates over time and depreciates each year.

Although classic cars have risen in value over the last 30 years, investing in a classic motor is not a guaranteed way to earn a decent return.

If you want to invest in cars, you need to find a vehicle that is the right fit in terms of cost and condition.

Most cars will never be an investment that will generate a profit as they lose value immediately after being driven off the dealership; however, classic cars gain value over time.

Cars with historical importance can become collectible, especially if they are rare and beautiful.

The car market mirrors the art market. It's an investment you enjoy aesthetically.

This is tangible personal property, and you will owe capital gains tax if you sell at a profit.

You can buy a new or almost new car because you think it will be collectible someday, but this is risky.

Advantages of car investment:
• Style and character
• Driving experience
• Personal enjoyment

Disadvantages of a car investment:
• Financial outlay
• Maintenance
• No mod-cons
• Depreciation

You can search for a classic car online.

# Art

Art has no correlation to the stock market, which means that paintings can go up in value even when the market crashes however art is a highly illiquid asset.

It can take years to have your art piece sold at auction so if you are going to invest in it, consider art investing a medium to long-term addition to your portfolio.

Art can be a risky investment. Artists and their work go in and out of style, affecting the resale value and return on investment.

Art acquisition comes with considerable extra costs, such as commissions and insurance. The most significant risk is that there is always a chance of forgery, theft, or damage.

You should work with an art investment advisor and you should abandon notions of what you like and don't like.

Jewellery from certain modern eras can attract higher prices. Art Deco jewellery from 1920 and 1930 is currently enjoying a resurgence.

Certain jewels and brands have held their value over time. Names such as Cartier and Van Cleef & Arpels are good examples of perceived quality.

Advantages of investing in jewellery:
• They are tangible assets
• They can't be hacked or erased
• They are portable

Disadvantages of investing in jewellery:
• Cost
• Storage
• They are not liquid assets
• They don't produce income or interest

You can purchase them in reputable stores or even in auctions.

## Wine

Fine wine matures once bottled and improves with age. Demand and interest in fine wine are growing around the world.

Types of wine are: white, red, rose, dessert of sweet and sparkling.

You can use a  merchant for his knowledge to help you source genuine good quality investment grade wine. It is strongly recommended that you seek advice when investing in wine as not all well-known wines are suitable for investment.

You are investing in an asset that has limited production but a huge global demand.

As it is an unregulated market, only buy from established merchants and ensure you get the expertise needed.

Short-term gains have been possible, but your investment should be viewed as mid to long-term. At least five years should be considered the norm, eight to ten years even better.

Only specific wines tend to accrue value, and they tend to be expensive.

Never buy from a wine investment company that cold calls you.

Only invest if you know what you are doing or you know someone you can trust with experience in dealing with fine wine.

Don't buy wine over 15 years old unless you know what you are doing, as the risk of fake wine is more significant with older wines.

Make sure the bottles of wine are in their original wooden case and are a complete set.

Advantages of investing in wine:
• Offers attractive returns
• Less volatile
• Global demand

Disadvantages of investing in wine:
• Lack of liquidity
• The high cost of storage
• High commission selling fee
• Fake wines
• Unregulated market

You can buy investment-grade wine from in-person auctions, online auctions, online wine exchange, specials stores, and vineyards.

## Commodities

Commodity funds invest in raw materials or primary agricultural products, known as commodities.

Supply, demand, and geopolitics all affect commodity prices.

Commodity funds deliver several benefits to investors:
• Portfolio diversification
• Protection against inflation. Commodities prices tend to rise with inflation, making it one of the few assets that benefit from inflation.
• Potential financial growth. Commodity prices rise and fall in line with supply and demand. The more a commodity is in demand, the higher its price will increase, delivering higher profits to the investor.

There are many different types of commodity funds, including:

- Index funds. These funds track an index that includes various commodity assets.
- Commodity funds. These funds invest directly in the commodity asset.
- Futures-based commodity funds. Invest in futures contracts without ever buying the actual commodity assets.

Commodities that are traded are typically sorted into four categories :
- Metals. Gold, silver, platinum, and copper. Gold has been traditionally a safe investment. When there is an increase in demand, the price of gold also goes up. It has successfully preserved wealth throughout thousands of generations. You can choose to hold bars or coins. There is no right or wrong answer. Gold is seen as a crucial part of any investment portfolio because it mitigates the risk that the rest of your investments will be subject to.
- Energy. Include crude oil, heating oil, natural gas, and gasoline.
- Livestock and meat
- Agriculture. Include corn, soybeans, wheat, rice, cocoa, coffee, cotton, and sugar.

One way to invest in commodities is through a futures contract. A futures contract is a legal agreement to buy or sell a particular commodity asset at a predetermined price at a specified time in the future.

The buyer of a futures contract is taking on the obligation to buy and receive the underlying commodity when the futures contract expires.

The seller is taking on the obligation to provide and deliver the underlying commodity at the contract's expiration date.

Advantages of investing in commodities:
• Diversification
• Potential returns
• Potential protection against inflation

Disadvantages of investing in commodities:
•Prices can be volatile
•It can be affected by world events

There are three ways to own commodities:
• Own the physical commodity itself
• Buy future contracts
• Buy through a mutual fund or ETF

# Conclusion

Now that you finished reading this book, I hope that you feel a little bit less scared about finance and that you can see how investment can help you grow your money.

You now know about the main investments, their pros, and cons, and you should start making a mental picture in your head of what investments would be the ones you would like to pursue.

The priority should be to ensure all debts are paid off and that you have an emergency fund with enough money in it to ensure you are prepared for any eventuality, without any issues.

Another necessary step would be to find a financial advisor who can guide you on your next step. Do not forget, as your money grows, so can your financial awareness and knowledge too.

Only invest what you can and feel comfortable with.

Cast your glance towards the future and start making plans to help you reach a more comfortable retirement outlook.

Congratulations! You are taking the key steps to a better life!

# Reference sites

www.investopedia.com

www.moneyadviceservice.org.uk

www.moneysavingexpert.com

www.thebalance.com

www.fidelity.com

# About the author

This is the second book written by Marcella Sersante. You can visit her online at author.to/author.

Her first book is called: A Customised Guide for Minimalism.